God
Gays
and Grace

God
Gays and
Grace

A book of teaching and testimony
on the gospel of Grace

Ken LaFleur

A Saint is not someone who does good.
A Saint is someone that knows
the goodness of God.

authorHOUSE®

AuthorHouse™
1663 Liberty Drive
Bloomington, IN 47403
www.authorhouse.com
Phone: 1-800-839-8640

First published by AuthorHouse   11/6/2009

ISBN: 978-1-4490-4425-1 (e)
ISBN: 978-1-4490-4424-4 (sc)
ISBN: 978-1-4490-4423-7 (hc)

Library of Congress Control Number: 2009911527

Printed in the United States of America
Bloomington, Indiana

This book is printed on acid-free paper.

Contents

Rex   Ken

In Tribute to my loving partner Rex
for encouraging me through
Ten years of writing these articles.

Ode to Rex

After 59 years of searching,
The Lord looked down on me,
And let this troubadour of song,
From loneliness finally be free.
He sent to me an angel,
And joy filled my soul,
A spirit filled basket of kindness he brought,
His gentleness for me he'd unfold.
He showed me how to except this world,
My brashness how to control,
And my anger that I had inside,

He melted away into gold.
I'd never met a man so sweet,
So gentle and so kind,
With tools of love he swept me away,
And soothed my soul and mind.
A gift he was to build me up,
My spirit encourage from fear,
To sing of the Lord, in spiritual tones,
In a voice made loud and clear.

The shadows today of life grow long,
Dark clouds are filling the sky,
A sign that his light's growing
dimmer each day,
And soon, we'll be saying good bye.
But I got to share a few thoughts with him,
Thoughts I carried in my minds eye,
A view of heaven, of beauty, and grace,
To share it makes my heart cry.
I see wisps of sweetness of energy fly,
Positive energy, through
Gods creation above,
And scenes of beauty an artist would know,
Never ending, a gift of Gods love.
The stars shimmer forth

brilliant colors they are,
and galaxies, wondrous beauty they bring,
singing songs in harmony,
joy, peace, and love,
sweet sounds of our heavenly king.

Thanks Rex for ten beautiful years

CHAPTER 1

You are gift in this moment of time.

*I*n experiencing our life we have seen, heard, emotionally felt, and absorbed many things. There have been tragedies, and there have been many blessings, all have been lessons in life. The tragedy's, heal and fade away, but the blessings change our life forever. During the blessings, we have experienced a glimpse of God, and that experience you can hide or you could share with others to bolster their faith. It is a gift that only you can share.

We are all cracked vessels and because of this many feel they are out of Gods favor and are not worthy of sharing their blessings. I want to tell you all now that it is through these imperfections, cracks in our vessel, that our spiritual light beams ever so brightly over a darkening world. You alone have the power to give strong testimony into faith, even though, like every person on earth you carry some darkness. Out of your darkness you can bring light into the world.

We are granted a number of days to live. For some maybe seventy years, some less time, some a little more. Where are you in your time? And are you aware that you are a gift to the world. How has God touched you? God touches us all no-matter how we have walked our life. And that spiritual touch, would you hide it under a basket, or would you share it so all could see, that bringing our darkness out into the light transforms our darkness into that shining ray of hope that the world so desperately needs.

Some times I wonder why the Christian way of life has not fixed the wrongs of the world , after all we have been at it for 2000 years. What is wrong? Could it be that Christians have not been honest with themselves, with others?

When I hear some one say, when I was a sinner I did thus and so, but now I am not a sinner, I think, its time to face reality. All things are bound by sin, but for Gods grace I have been forgiven. And that healing grace carries me from day to day. Cleansing my spirit moment to moment. The truth is we are all sinners and without Faith in the cleansing power of God's grace every one would be lost. It is not in the plan of God that he loose one.

No one can come to me unless the father calls him, and any that he calls I will not lose. I am sure that all, at one time in there life have felt the call of the Father, it's a spiritual call that resounds in your inner being, a longing in your heart to come before the lord and let him comfort you, a longing to have the wounds of life washed and cleansed, a longing to be to be clean and whole in spirit. There is no place to get that in this world, only by Grace through the healing power of Jesus.

So, once again I ask where are you in your life, are you just ambling along trapped in your darkness or are you ready to step out in courage and without fear of being exposed, to let out that goodness in your soul, out through the cracks in your vessel and allow the truth, and brilliant light of the spirit to shine, lighting the darkness, and being a beacon for all to see?

There is a wonderful song by the Weston Priory that sums it all up. "Won't you take the time, to come and heal my friend, then I'll know there is a reason to believe in you."

You are a gift in this moment of time.

CHAPTER 2

Church life 101

Why do we have church? As the church gathers on Sundays, one by one a gift arrives. Each one a unique special precious one of a kind gift from the Lord. Each is a piece of the Body, that I call Church. As we gather the Body strengthens, and is capable of accomplishing many things. The most awesome of which is the presence of God in its mist. The Church, or the Body of Christ gathered, is the core of our community. Here people Gay or Straight, that are searching for their way to God, can come together and be affirmed by the strength of the Body. New members can feel the presence of God, and feel love, perhaps for the first time. Each one of us is a cracked earthen vessel, passing through a moment of time, and from each crack radiates the wondrous light of your spirit. Your special gift, that shines out to minister and heal, anoint and praise, sing and prophecy. This is how the Body is affirmed. The sanctuary is a retreat. Where we can come and find a neutral place. A place that is isolated from the world and a place where you can reach out and experience the grace of the Lord. Fellowship, especially if you are a gay person, most likely, was a non existent spiritual experience. But with the church we find that it is possible to have a wonderful full experience with God. There are plenty of gay people that will share their lives and support you along your way. I know you would not have stayed with this letter this far if you were not called by God. And I know your spirit will never be filled unless you pursue his calling.

I have not yet found the spot or the activity at the Ramrod or the Eagle where I am at peace and filled with gratitude like I feel when I'm in the presence of God. Why? Because, it's just not there. When you go to the Ramrod you get Ramrod, when you do Eagle you get Eagle. But when it's your time to come to the

Lord, the starting place is here in Church, with the gathering of all these Saints. You know that a Saint is not a person that does good, but a Saint is a person that knows the goodness of God. This Church has embarked on a long overdue mission. A mission to bring God to the Gay community. John6:3-7 says, "All that the Father gives to me shall come to me. No one who comes shall I ever reject". You may get rejected at Chardee's or the Alibi, but you will not be rejected here. This is your place to grow, this is the place where you can begin to fill that hollow empty feeling that you have experienced. And this is why we have Church.

What is the reason's for coming to Church? It' was best said by Leo Biscallia, when he was asked " Why do you need love", His reply was " because I leak, and I need to be refilled". We to as Christians need to be refilled. The world has it's way of obscuring the clarity of our memories. Through anger, deception, fantasy, over crowding, you name it and it's there to work on us. This is one reason to come to church. (We leak.) There is another reason too, (other people leak), and they need to be renewed, and guess what! You may have just the spiritual gift that they need to fill them. That is called Affirmation. Here is a guarantee, you will not find much affirmation if any, out in the world. We need the spiritual gifts, that are carried by our brothers and sisters to renew us. No one person has them all, but together we as the Body do have them all.

What are the gifts of the spirit that we are talking about? They are, Knowledge, Faith, Healing, Miraculous powers, Prophecy, Distinguishing Spirits, and Tongues. And they are all together when we are gathered as the body of Christ. Here is fertile ground for growing in the Spirit.

What should we expect from a church? I can only tell you from my own testimony, so here it is. I had bolted away from my old Church, and 12 years had slipped by. I came back in when I found a Church that loved me. What an experience it was. It was like I had entered a room filled with unconditional love. The presence of God was overwhelming. It was awesome, and I new I had come home. People were singing praise's to the Lord, and the hall was swept in the sweet sent of the spirit. Hundreds of people were singing in tongues, testimonies of experiences were being shared, prophecy and interpretation of tongues, people healed before our very eyes, whole sections of the church slain in the spirit at one time. I new I was in a very special place, and I new that I wanted more than anything to be able to return again. I had so far to go, I was so damaged from priests that just didn't know, or they were to afraid to step out in faith to tell me the truth. But I new from that experience, that God loved me very much, and he was not going to lose me again. I new I had a gift for music and he called me into ministry. There I grew, sang, was ministered too, and ministered to others. Awesome, just awesome were the experiences of love and healing I was shown. It all happened because a community said yes, Lord we will do it what ever it takes. Teaching classes were set up to teach life in the Spirit. Obscure people became anointed gifted speakers, and out of a prayer meeting of five people, did a community of seven hundred arise. That is what we are called to do for the Gay community. What is your responsibility in a church? To <u>love</u> one another as God loves us. That is with an unconditional love. <u>Understanding</u>, taking the time to know people, their hurts and their dreams, where they are going with their lives. <u>Support</u>, not only in financial support but be willing to support the Ministries. <u>Honesty</u>, have deep open and meaningful relationships with each other. <u>Ministries</u>, Get involved you are gifted in so many ways. This is the place, where God wants you to share your gifted-ness.

CHAPTER 3

Living again, new and whole.

*S*o many of us who are coming back to church didn't feel worthy to come before the Lord. And some of us didn't feel worthy to pray either. Some of us are here to find our way, and some come here because they feel the presence of God within this community. Most of us are not here to find Religion, since religion has hurt many of us. So what are we looking for? Could it be that we are searching for a spiritual reunion with God? A feeling of oneness with our creator, if the later is why you are here, than that is reason #1 to keep returning.

Many have come and gone through these doors. Many have gone on to develop their ministries and spread the good news, or bring music to those that need ministering through their gift. Many have moved away, and the Lord has called many home. And many have left still searching, because they have not focused on <u>their</u> personal walk with God.

I choose to stay. Though is has been a very rocky road that I have traveled spiritually in my search for God, and many of those in there religious places that could have helped me have scarred me badly, yet I choose to stay.

You might ask me why? I can only tell you that things are revealed to you as you walk along your way in life. I was almost 50 years old before it was put together for me.

I thought I had made a spiritual connection when I was in the Charismatic Renewal, I was involved, and living in the spirit yet I truly did not comprehend God. It wasn't until I had a paradigm shift in my spirituality, a shift away from the Old Testament to the new, specifically accepting the gospel of grace.

And what is the Gospel of Grace? It teaches us that Jesus paid the price, the whole price for our justification in God's eyes for the sins of the past, present, and future. <u>This is the gift.</u>

<u>The Gift of Grace</u>. There was nothing I could do or give that would be enough to pay for this wonderful gift, all I had to do was to accept it for it to be mine. Yes! I had to learn to accept the gift of Grace like a kid getting a Christmas present from Mom and Dad. For the first time in 50 years I could bring myself, in my wholeness, just as I truly am, a Gay man, joyfully into the presence of the Lord. Washed clean with grace and still me.

Being finally at home, and knowing all is well here, in the presence of God, spiritually reunited, I can now finally grow into what God wants. I can let go of the stumbling blocks, and hangup's that I've had, that prevented me from fully engaging in the call of ministry.

Being surrounded buy a living spiritual church has set me free. Letting me hear the healing words of the Lord through them has put my soul at peace. This could even be reason #2 to stay on.

One last thought I would like to leave with this teaching is, a Saint is not a person that does good. A Saint is a person that knows the goodness of God.

CHAPTER 4

Living Again, finding your holiness.

I'll bet within the range of this teaching, there are those that have truly been seeking a way to be reunited with the Lord, but have been abruptly knocked of the track of success by those that have said "gay people" will never see God.

But that is not the word of God. As I recall it Jesus said, "anyone, anyone that believes in me shall have everlasting life", and anyone the father send's to me I shall not loose". Doesn't that sound like a one on one thing? Where docs the "church" get the Gate keeper job as to who can be with the Lord, and how could any church exclude a living soul in search of the Lord?

You can come into the presence of the Lord just as you are a gay person. You can tell him in you own words, "I love you Lord, and I place my eternity in your hands Jesus". It's all sincere prayer. This is the courageous first steps of a person starting his/her spiritual walk, the opening of the door to being reunited, your spirit with the Lord. <u>This is good news</u>.

The most unfortunate things working against the gay person seeking to be reunited with God today is old indoctrinations, and teachings of the legalistic church. St Paul totally cleared this up in Galatians. Gal:3-11 St Paul said, "it should be obvious that no one is justified in God's sight by the law, for the just man shall live by faith. Gal:4-23 Before faith came, we were under the constraint of the law, locked in until the faith that was coming was revealed. In other words the law was our monitor until Christ came to bring about our Justification. But now that faith is here we are no longer in the monitors charge. All that have been baptized into Christ have clothed yourselves in him.

Most of the Gay community has never had the chance to focus in on a walk with the Lord.

Many feel the guilt of previous teachings, and have resolved themselves outcasts from a spiritual life. There is nothing further from the truth then this. If you can muster up your faith, telling the Lord you love him, and place your eternity in his hands, and courageously take the first steps, you will be on your way, you will feel right in your spirit, peace will enter your soul, and you will be right with God, and you will choose to say, I am going to stay. Yes! I am blessed by living the Gospel of Grace, and I can now focus on a spiritual life even though I am gay.

Now for the first time in your adult life you can take a look at the Two Commandments that Jesus gave us. #1 To love God with your whole heart mind and soul. #2 To love your neighbor as God loves you. This wisdom and strength leads us onward in our walk with him.

I will leave you with this thought, God walks with you in peace. He has opened your eyes to see, gave you a clear mind to analyze what you have heard, and steadfast courage to take another step tomorrow. This is the reason to stay on in a spiritual community, and even bring someone you love with you when you come back.

CHAPTER 5

Living Again, Walking Through Life.

I just can't imagine how it could be, that intelligent people which have had the key for happiness for two thousand years, could bring the world to such a state that we find it in today.

The only thing I can ascribe it too is, that all the Leaders must have been Fundamentalists, or all the Elders must have been on testosterone boosters or something, because of the stance they took as rulers.

Consider this:

Instead of pursuing power by saying
"THOU SALT NOT",
THEY COULD HAVE SAID,
" IF YOU LOVED ME YOU ",
Would love the Lord alone.
wouldn't worship idol's.

wouldn't worship false Gods.
wouldn't take God's name in vain.
Would keep the Sabbath holy.
Would honor your mom and dad.
Wouldn't kill me.
Wouldn't have sex with my partner.
Wouldn't steal my stuff.
Wouldn't bear false wittiness.
Wouldn't desire my belongings.

Just think of it, The revelation of the millenniums and we're still, to this day, missing it, all because of a power trip. When will the legalistic church wake up.

Sometime things just aren't clear until you've gotten a few grey hairs in your head, but when you see or hear a revelation you have to yell it out from the mountain top.

All those (as Mother Theresa calls them suggestions) would have made an astounding difference in the world as we know it today.

We would love ourselves just as we are. We would have loved others as we loved our selves. We would have been a Holy People.

We would take care of our ageing parents. We wouldn't have murder every where. We wouldn't be having sex with our neighbors partner. We wouldn't steal each others stuff. We wouldn't lie. And we wouldn't desire our neighbors stuff.

I guess you could say that if we had this attitude we would be living a "Christian life," and we wouldn't have Christian leaders breeding hate to those that are different then themselves. Pointing the Bible at others like a weapon.

Somehow the truth got twisted, and the only way that it is going to work out, is that we must return to the Masters plan.

It really is not a hard thing to do, but the entire church needs to wake up and commit to reevaluating itself, but of course some must swallow their pride and say that I was wrong .

Here is the way it should be done. We must accept fully, and live by, the two commandments that the Lord gave us. This is a complete set of directions for a successful society. And includes all the teachings of the Prophets.

I leave you with this. Love your God with your whole heart, and the second is like it . Love one another as I have loved you.

CHAPTER 6

Living Again, Completing the Walk.

$\mathcal{A}$s I sit here thinking about this walk in spiritual life, I wonder why I so often relied on those around me to fill my life. Specially, to form my spiritual life. I think it was to give me a starting place. Our basic walk in religion was to give us a chance to learn through others, a basic understanding of God. That is how I see the purpose of religion, basic training.

God has gifted us all with many Chrism's, each one a beautiful gift, and only found in you. When that special gift of yours, mixes with the gifts of others, and flows in unconditional love towards community, that's where you will find Church.

When you get religion. What are you going do with it? It's just a starting place. The answer is to grow into your own spirituality. And as you grow into that spirituality, and get reunited with God, you will be experiencing a wholeness and sense of peace, and the presence of God in your life.

We will always need the basic Church, because here is the starting place for those searching for there God, but that is not the end of your spiritual journey. Your walk on in the spirit will ever bring you closer to God, and stronger in the spirit. We have to become strong in our walk in the spirit. We have to begin to be able to walk alone with him feeling safe and secure, because in the end, only he will walk off with us in death. Neither the Church in all it's goodness, nor the Pastors nor your friends will be able to continue on and comfort you, in your eternal walk.

CHAPTER 7

Earthen vessels.

In reflecting over my life, I think about the people that I have met, experienced, or seen that have positively affected my life spiritually. I also have images of those that adversly affected me spiritually as well. The People that have adversly affected me are what I would call the polished pots. They are those that posture themselves to the world as holy leaders. Some are Pope's, Cardinals, and Bishops, some are Televangelist, some are non-flexible lay people, some are Bible thumping Evangelist. They are the ones that insist their way is the only way to have a relationship with God. Some times I have to laugh at some of their ridiculous costumes, massive makeup jobs, hairdos, and projected righteousness. Some times their delivery is so strange, it's obvious they haven't a clue about spiritual living. I walked into a Men's room on a recent trip through the south, and there in the stall was a scratched in sign that said Jesus is watching you. Didn't he know, he was watching him too, while he defaced public property? Well, I'm sure you have the jist of those folk. But the earthen vessels, the quiet ones with loving hearts, unglamorous non-pretentious, poor some time, but caring people with a clear understanding that they are not perfect, having faults, and admit they have fissures in there lives, they are the cracked earthen vessels of God. And these are the ones that have that spiritual light blazing away inside them. When you take a polished pot into the darkness it will disappear because there is no light. On the other hand when a cracked earthen vessel with an internal spiritual light goes into the darkness it beams through the cracks from the light that burns from within. When I work from the faults that are within me, or when I begin to own up to my real self, and I bring that whole self into the presence of God, there is a wonderful anointing that happens. My personhood, mental, physical, and spiritual, are brought into harmony with God, and when I step out in faith to minister, truth, and honesty, seem to strike home with all. There is no pretense in ministering; it is a flow that pours out through the Holy Spirit and ministers to the very soul of a person in need of healing. Polished pots may not be anointed to do the job. So my friends it is very important to bring yourself before God as you are. You may be very surprised at the work the spirit will call you to do.

Once on a retreat I felt the call to go down to chapel, it was really late into the night. A candle was burning and the Eucerist was out on display. I just sat there and was engulfed in Gods presence. After a while a lady came in and she was very distressed and lay prostrate before the Lord, and she cried. I silently lifted her up in prayer and she came over to me and told me that she had done things that would never be forgiven. She talked for a long time. I told her that all sins of mankind would be forgiven, except blasphemy against the Holy

Spirit. I could feel the peace settle on her and I left. You never know when you will be called to minister, but you can not minister if you are not whole and in union with God. In union with God does not mean perfect, or polished pots. It means that God knows you, all of you, as that earthen vessel.

CHAPTER 8

Encouraging words.

Thessalonians2:13 We are bound to thank God for you always, beloved brothers/Sisters in the Lord, because you are the first fruits of those whom God has chosen for salvation. Thessalonians2:14 He called you through our preaching of the "Good news" (The Gospel of Grace) so that you might achieve the glory of our lord Jesus Christ. Thessalonians3:5 May the Lord rule in your hearts in the love of God and the constancy of Christ.

You are a truly blessed people, because through your Teaching and Testimony, you may be the first persons to have reached so deeply into the gay community's soul. You let our community know that God truly loves us.

You all have brought special spiritual gifts. Through your efforts we are becoming a part of the body of Christ (Church). You can test these gifts of the spirit buy the fruit it produces. And the fruit brothers/sisters are those that have heard the Gospel of Grace and renewed their faith through you, and are coming home to God just as they are, The gay, loving, caring, sharing, and holy, unique, special, precious, children of God...

CHAPTER 9

A Gay Mans View of Relating to God in Heaven, God on earth, and God's Holy Spirit

ver the past 6 decades I have had to wrestle with how I see God. It's not a new paradox, even Leonardo DeVinci found himself there, pondering this very thought. It is hard for me to see Him as a human being, or super human being, for what human form could have created the universe and beyond. Even though Jesus called him Father when he said, "If you know me then you also know The Father".

Until recently I have always found it easier to relate to Jesus and the Holy Spirit, probably because I relate to His healing gift of grace, and have felt the presence of the Holy Spirit in my life.

But for me there was always been something missing in theology, and that is, what is the relationship here? What is the connecting emulsion or aggregate that ties this all together? At long last I am coming to peace with it all.

In my relationship with the Holy Spirit, the communication is in spiritual thought in prayer. This process use's spiritual energy. I believe that this energy flows as a natural phenomenon, both ways, to us and from us. When we are in the presence of The Holy Spirit, when we are at prayer, when we minister through healing, and inspired by Spiritual living teachings, we experience this Positive Spiritual Energy.

In my relationship with Jesus, He is the Messiah (Savior) the Devine Messenger, and son of God, and that is the relationship I have with him, but I would like to get the language out of the known religious vernacular and talk about this in modern every day terms.

How do I relate to Jesus? Well, I have my Faith in him. I have placed my eternity in his hands. "He that believes in me shall have eternal life." And, I have now let go of all my guilt, and accept the wonder of the gift of his grace. Yes, now I can give to him from my very core, a steady flow of positive spiritual energy flowing toward him and, through him caring for me, and dying for <u>all</u> my faults, past, present, and future, he has replenished my soul with more positive spiritual energy.

How did Jesus relate with his "Father"? He knew "The Father", placed his faith and trust in "The Father", which made him one in spirit and, the positive spiritual energies could flow to "The Father" and a return flow to Jesus refilling his spiritual personhood. The guiltless unobstructed flows of energy from "The Father" to Jesus, is probably the same force that allowed the miracles to happen and, caused the resurrection.

Now, the big question is how do I relate to "The Father"?

Well, I don't see him up in the control room pushing buttons causing hurricanes as some have suggested. No! That's not my God. My God is running the universe as we know it and beyond, and there may be more universe's out there he is running. We have no idea how big this creation is. God is keeping the balance of all things in spiritual harmony, I don't have a picture in my mind of what "The Father" looks like, or if he looks like anything at all, but the thing that sticks with me the most is the unity in which my being is in tune with "him". As long as I live in positive spiritual energy (in faith & grace), my soul is illuminated and bathed in his love and acceptance.

Now that I have shared that with you, I would like to share a vision I had the other night.

I live in the sub-tropics, and as night was falling the sky turning to pitch black, yet the yard was still some what illuminated, I had a thought of what the last moments of life would be like for me. How would I receive this last moment?

I could feel the flow of wonderfully colored energy run from me, and I could see it flow and focus on the Jesus that I have come to love. The river of spiritual energy flowed through him magnified and went straight out to the universe, where I could see the creation and majesty of God, but It did not stop. It flew into the darkness and I said, Lord is there to much negative energy in me? I was reassured with a bathing of loving spiritual energy, and came back toward the beautiful vision of creation. A word of knowledge, and of understanding came over me of the scripture when Jesus said, "in my fathers house there are many mansions". Look for yourself at all the constellations, star systems, nebulas. It's more beauty then can be beheld. "Welcome Home, your spiritual energy is in balance with me, The Father"..

CHAPTER 10

Gay Evangelism.

There are so many wonderful gay and lesbian people out in this world that have been torn from there religion for various reasons, some from Pastors that have missed their mark in teaching love, tolerance, and compassion. Some because of religious dogma and others because of Community rejection. So where are they now?

They are in life's solitude, searching for a new grip on life. Some, look into bars for some one to help stabilize there life. Some, look into cruising, and some, go into there darkness for cover and protection. But all are searching for the truth and meaning for there lives. Every one of them are internally searching. When we as spiritual people finally understand this fact, some thing becomes apparently clear to us, we are stewards of a great gift.

What is this great gift that we have been so blessed with? Its that we have found a loving family, a community of spiritual brothers and sisters that care, a community that lifts us up out of life's solitude and encourages us to once again trust and believe. A community that lifts us up from disappointment and despair, and shows us, a cleansing spiritual experience that heals and revitalizes us. You know this is true, we all have experienced this here in this church.

But how did you ever get here? How did you find your way here? For most I'm sure, that someone cared enough to tell you about this place. Maybe showed you the way here, or raised your interest to come and see for yourself. <u>This is Gay Evangelism</u>. Nothing hard about that, it's just pointing the way. There is no theology required, that is not the call of evangelism, we have teachers and pastors and many ministries for that, as evangelist we are simply to point the way.

When we wanted to joined this church we promised to share our "Time Talent and Treasure", this is all stewardship. Sharing with others outside the community about the loving family you found inside, is using your "Time" well, an easy way to exercise your stewardship. The easiest way for me to Evangelize is to carry a few church business cards with me, and to show my love by sharing and pointing the way, give that inquiring person a card and let God do the rest.

CHAPTER 11

Gay History of Ken on coming out and being visible.

I was raised as a girl till I was 5 ½ yrs old. That was the custom in the early forties if a Mom wanted a girl she just dressed her baby that way. I had really long blond wavy hair and was treated like a girl. I adored my older brother.

By the time I was seven I knew I found the boys more interesting than the girls, and it was that way all through my adolescence. In high school I only dated one girl and also enjoyed a male relationship for those years. At seventeen I went into the service. When the Navy realized I was gay at the age of twenty they tossed me in the Brig, and discharged me with an Undesirable Discharge, and the career I had chosen to work in was destroyed.

Thinking that I had made a wreck out of my life, I said I have to change my ways. I returned home and married the only girl I ever dated. We had two kids and I tried to live a straight life till I realized that my dreams were never to be for-filled. Years went buy with a few occasional gay trysts.

At age thirty five I had become deeply involved in the Catholic Charismatic Renewal, and felt somewhat straight, until when returning off a retreat we came out onto the lobby of the retreat house and there were two beautiful men in leotards there, and I could feel the rush of my gay personhood flood in, and I knew then I was always to be a gay person.

Time passed and through the years I would continue to have the very occasional gay tryst. It was like a balm that soothed my wholeness of being. My wife knew I was a gay person,

(I had shared some thoughts with her), but we struggled on and raised the kids, and later moved to Florida.

We separate after 35 years of marriage, and I found I could not return to the church that had been my bedrock foundation. I was a spirit filled person suddenly with out a church. At that point I decided that I would never be untrue to my self again, and came out of the closet, and started searching for a church that I was comfortable with. One requirement for the church would be that my guitar was welcome and that I could sing in the spirit and live in wholeness as a gay person. I arrived at C.O.S. (Church of Our Savior MCC) in 1996. Here I found a home and a loving spiritual family.

I met a person that made me feel welcome here. I was a little timid of her at first because she was big strong and decisive in her actions, but Pat Santry loved me from the start as a gay person, and she made sure that I fit in. After a while she found out I was into music, and I was drafted into the choir.

It took a long time for me to heal from a broken marriage, the loss of friends and family, and a church that was no longer right for me, and I quietly settled down at C.O.S. As time passed I knew I had to start using all the spiritual Gifts that were safely tucked away inside of me. Gifts that God had given to me as he walked with me all through the years.

Three years had now gone by, and I had been alone with out a companion, as I climbed up the stairs of the beach pavilion one night I said, Lord I need a mate for my life, and just three weeks later I met my soul mate Rex. We are on our sixth year now of our relationship. Our lives are whole, our spirituality is whole, and our ministries bear fruit.

We have been blessed in so many ways. A loving church, wonderful friends, loving and accepting neighbors, and a new spiritual family. As an openly gay couple we faced the world in wholeness. We minister and serve the local community sharing the gifts that God has given to us. The "Fundamentalist unloving church" would have us living in darkness and shame, but we walk in God's grace, in the light, and reflecting the goodness of God. We are your Musicians to sooth your soul, your Artists bringing you beauty, your Nurses comforting your sick. We are the Teachers that bring understanding and knowledge. We are the Fireman that die in falling buildings protecting you. We are soldiers that are fighting for your freedom, and we are a voting minority struggling with Legislators for equality. We are part of the fabric of life that warms and protects the world you live in. Yes, we are even your brothers and sisters. Your sons and your daughters with an out stretched hand in love. Waiting for your out stretched hand giving love.

I encouraging you to come out, be visible for we are still yearning to be free.

The Beginning.

CHAPTER 12

Feelings, truthfulness, understanding, = wisdom 101

od touches me. Some times He'll touch me at times I don't expect, like tonight while I was under a nice hot shower. Some times He will get my attention, some times He doesn't, but God has allowed my heart to stay always open, and when He is persistent I have to respond.

I have a revelation for you He said, as you walk your way through this life, you have only the moment you're in, to be Me for those that surround you. From your view, you can look out into this world and see in timely fashion. You have eyes of the present, that can see the needs of this world that you live in. In your living experience you have seen and recognized the pain of the hearts, that all people are living through. You have seen the masks of men that hide the inner sorrow of their souls, and you can see through to their souls and know this is the time I should step in and minister. But how many times we have turned away. It was easier that way, not so much of a load. So you left with the gifts of the healing still locked inside you.

My thought for the night was, that at the end of this dash through life, how did you spend the wealth of talent that was gifted to you. Were you a good steward of my gifts? Did you exercise your talent? Or did the gifts dry on the vine and fade away?

Have we built our lives on friends, acquaintances, things, jobs, and rules and regulations? Where is your security?

These things disappear from our lives on this dash through life. The friends go their way in time, and acquaintances even faster disappear. Jobs come and go and what guides us onward. The rules and regulations are just that, and they have no feeling. They guide but never heal. No, the one thing that stays constantly in my life, is the gift of grace. When do we receive the gift of grace?

When we except our own personhood and wholeness in ourselves, and bring our total self with our wholeness of being (in faith) before the Lord and say, "Here I am lord, would you accept me as I am", so that I can be with you. would you take the time to hold me in your arms and comfort me,   Lord, each time you do that, you show me all the things I thought were darkness that have been in my life, were actually brilliant beams of light to be used to show the way.

I realize, that in this dash through life Lord, all the goodies are going to fade away, loving partners die, friends, and jobs disappear, we can not hold it all, its really not ours to hold, try as we might we can not hold it. Why can't we hold it?

Because it belongs to the world. The things that we know today, will be soon be in the past. We are people of the present. So, all these thoughts tonight brings me to this realization.

Living through this present moment, when it comes time to leave this life, the one treasure I will take with me, will be the grace that God has shared with me. The only thing that mattered above all through this life was, that I knew ahead of time, that life is only between you and I Lord.

Life is between you and I. We will all cross over alone with out a parade of friends, but grace will carry us over together Lord. The life long gift of grace.

CHAPTER 13

Of Teaching and Testimony

had a teacher of bookkeeping when I was in the 10th grade, She was of a round non descript short stature, and her face was set like a flint. She ran the class with the finesse of a drill Sergeant. It looked like it was going to be a tough semester.

To top off this radiant atmosphere, she had my older brother two years before, and my older sister three years before that. The first day I entered the room she looked at me and said LaFleur sit down. I had your brother and your sister in this class, and your first mistake your out the door. I got an (F) FAILURE going through the first two terms, and left the class. There are Teachers that teach because its there job. Time passes, 40 years later, I was on a retreat with the men from my church, and this year John was the retreat master. You have to picture John, BIG man, I mean 290 lb big, a fullback. He had been many things in his life. A Bar bouncer, a collection person "so to speak," mean, nasty and rough jobs, and he wasn't the type of guy you would want to push around. But John had a conversion experience. He was going to teach us about the love of Jesus. He knew and loved the chance to share what he had experienced, He had become a man that was full of love and care and tenderness. When John stood up and started his teaching, he didn't stop for three days.

We were spellbound. There are teachers, and there are teachers. When John spoke, he spoke through his heart, through his experience, through personal things. He didn't care if he and some of his experiences were laughed at, some were hilariously funny. One time he stepped into an elevator in a hotel lobby and the floor fell out and he fell into the elevator pit, but the way John told it, it was outrageously funny. Some of his testimony was tragic, but John shared what was in him personally. To me, the drill Sergeant was a clanging bell that accomplished nothing. Where John was a soothing balm that healed the soul. John was giving testimony. He was telling his story. He was not a fake, he poured out his story for three days and we would have listened a whole week because it resonated truth within us. Telling his story was a gift that only he had. He was the expert and only he could tell it. Testimony's are without a doubt the best teaching tool we have. And "your" story is an important gift to share with this community. Your personal testimony is the place where you have the spiritual gift of "Teacher." I have shared with you some of my story. It comes in bunches and I don't remember it all, until someone strikes a cord in their (testimony) story, and another part of my story comes up from deep within. This is how we share our gifts and affirm the church.

While we are in this quiet time wont you share how you as a gay person became intimate in your relationship with the Lord. This community needs to hear it, and so don't I. As your story memories come up through this retreat, please, please jot them down and share them with us. This is the healing balm from inside your heart, These testimonies are the spirit speaking and calling to each of us..

CHAPTER 14

Your Testimony.

This is a special growing experience for you. This is where you hear your story, from deep down with in. Share with us your testimony where God has touched your lives. It's an interesting and learning experience, because each time you tell your story, you'll find a little variation in it, and after you have told it many times you'll start to get to the core being of who you are. You'll get to understand how blessed you've been, and just how many times that you've been graced by the Lord. It truly is amazing the things you hear, and the responses you get. One time I was on a retreat, and we were on an Emmaus walk.

(That's when two people pair up and walk with the Lord and share from within how

God has touched them.) I was sharing with a very macho type person. And about half way through the walk, I had to tell him that I was a gay person. It was just burning in side me, and it had to come out, and it had to come out to him. Why? I guess the spirit was pulling on me. Any way when I came out and told him, he didn't say anything for about ten minutes. Then he turned to me and said, "Ken my brother I have loved you for a long time, but I must tell you something. It's not that straight men hate gay men, it's that you hit a cord in us that scares us. It scares us because we are so much like you, and we are afraid that we could be you." He said 'we are all right on the edge of being gay. We've never experienced it, and it frightens the heck out of us." Nothing more needed to be said, and we continued walking in meditation for the rest of the hour. But, on that Emaus walk God had opened the door and revealed a gift of understanding between us....

CHAPTER 15

The Great Perversion

The great perversion my brothers and sisters is not how we as gay men and women act, (which needs to be addressed but in another teaching) no, rather it is that men in the name of God have turned the word of God from being directed inward to heal and minister to our own spirit, to turning it outward, forcing guilt, anxiety, fear, control, and ultimately separation from God himself. It is said, that faith comes from hearing, and that is true, But what are we hearing? Is it the Gospel of Grace as taught by our Lord, or is it the gospel of fear, unworthiness, and subjectitude as taught buy the Pharisees. I am afraid my friend that through the last few centuries, we have not heard the gospel of Grace.

The gospel of grace heals and unites us with God. It makes our spirit sing with joy and leap with delight as we become one with the creator, as we come into Gods presence. The gospel of Grace does not create fear, nor does it drive men against men. It does not instill hate, resulting in hate crimes, nor does it rush to judgment of others. The gospel of grace does not separate one segment of society from another. The gospel of grace is the balm that makes our spirit whole. A prophetic word, "Within your very own lifetime you will see the temples that PASTORS have built for themselves empty out, as GOD revives his gospel of grace. A Shepherd knows his sheep and they know him. They listen as he calls each one by his own name. The temples of the LORD will fill to overflowing as the word of Gods grace is heard."

CHAPTER 16

Serving one another in love.

y brothers and sisters, I ask you to bear with me through this teaching, cause it isn't easy to write. Let's go back now a bit, to the teaching on Knowing you are justified. In Gal:5-13 it say's, my brothers, remember that you have been called to live in freedom, but not a freedom that gives free reign to the flesh. Out of love, place yourselves at one an others service. The whole law has found its fulfillment in the following saying: "you shall love your neighbor as yourself." Don't choke on this let me explain. What St. Paul is saying here is, (aaaahem) here we go. You are called away from prostituting yourself to gain affection. I know it's hard under the situation that our community has been forced to live under, and

I know that in finding a mate we are forced unlike the heterosexual folk, to look in places that are safe for our sub culture. (I must ad here, that it is only a sub culture because we've been driven there as I explained in a previous teaching). We need to make the opportunity to find our loved one, and that isn't easy. But let me tell you a story.

I had come out of a 35 year marriage. And I had been living alone for three years. I had looked for my lover to come out of the MCC church where I worship, but alas he was not there. Finally in desperation early one morning while I was cruising on the beach I said, "this Lord is not where you want me to be", and as I climbed the stairs to the beach pavilion, I came to the lord and said, "please Lord I cant live like this I need a mate, please send him to me". I left a clear honest very explicit message on the boards at A.O.L over 50 , and within three weeks my lover answered. It was a perfect match. God knows better then we do what it is we really need. My lover is my age. We have similar memory's, He's just what I needed. I consider my lover a gift from the

Lord, and a joy to my life. We are together five years now, and are every bit as solid as husband and wife could ever be. We tested for HIV, and six months later tested again before having unprotected sex. It was surely the way it was supposed to be for me. Our community is killing itself having sex in the bizarre places of yesteryear. Living together as a couple openly gay has been wonderful to us. Our neighbors have figured out that were a couple, we haven't had to yell it out, and we didn't have to act up on the streets. We are all entitled to enjoy the wonderful fetishes that we share. Heterosexual couples have there own fetishes, YES!! They do. I guess the bottom line is, I'm trying to tell you, fall in love, treat each other as man and wife. Don't service the whole community, you'll get sick, and that is not what God has called you for. You of all people are the gifted ones, the Artists the Musicians, the Story tellers. You bring joy to life through your talent and gifts. Service each another in love, the lust part will diminish as our community comes up from under ground, and we will be able to find our true love easier in the future..

C H A P T E R 1 7

What would Jesus do to minister to the Gay community?

When Jesus walked through life and ministered, His Ministry was unconventional for the times. He didn't try to find the outcast's by hanging out with the Leadership of the Church. No, He knew they wouldn't be there. They had split and run away from any place that was uncomfortable or painful to them. Whether it was the Church, Family, or Society. Jesus new that in order to collect his people he had to go to them, to where they were. Jesus had to hang out with Ragamuffins. He knew that those who were outcast's would seek out small bands of there own kind for acceptance, love, compassion, and protection. The main line Church with it's moralistic values, Family's with their pride, and Society with it's judgments, had driven the outcast's underground. The Church had looked at them as unrepentant sinners. There family's had looked at them as bringing on shame. And the (upstanding) Pillars of society trashed them as outcast's. All had missed the message of Jesus, to live a loving and spiritual life. In order for us to bring home our Gay community to God, we all have to come to grips with who we are and why we have felt hurt. Here it is in a nutshell, Rejection, Loneliness, Pain, and Fear.

To bring our family home to God, we ourselves need to realize that we are all made to the Masters plan. We are Unique, Special, One of a kind, Precious children of God. We all feel the need to be made welcome just as we are, within the church community.

And this is where this teaching begins. If Jesus were to walk into a gay haunt today, he might ask why are you here, or what are you looking for tonight. The answer might be I'm looking for a playmate or a sex partner. But if he were to pursue the conversation, he would most likely find a lonely person, that in shear frustration, was just reaching out for the love and compassion that most of the world enjoy's. He might find that this person was starving for affection, of a person of his or her own nature, or he might find a "flamer" that was acting out the feelings of anger and resentment. Not one of these things makes a bad person. It just shows a dire need of love that is scarce to acquire. Not knowing where to find this, we are forced to look in the most bizarre places. Alcohol, Drugs, Bar's, Parks, Gym's Club rooms, ect. Each time an encounter is made the self image goes down, and after a while, there is no self image. We feel unworthy of anything, much less being in the presence of God. And when we've reached out to the Church, well, they want to fix us. My brothers and sisters, we have all been there haven't we. It is time to call your family out of the darkness. It is time to share the true Gospel of Grace. It is time to come out for the second time. Coming out to the gay community as a "gay Christian" is a requirement of living a gay Christian life. If you love your family you will want them to come out of there pain. Being honest and open is risky business. But the price of leaving your gay family in loneliness, rejection, fear, and pain is worth this price. Jesus did it for all, shouldn't we continue on? We as the "gay Church" may be the only Jesus that the Gay world might get to see ever. We have only this moment in time to open up and share. Look deep into the person, see what's in there. Become a listener. The only way a person can hear his or her story is to tell it. Lots of nice people have never heard there story. There story is there testimony. Wouldn't it be great if it ended , "and I came into the presence of the Lord and was accepted just as I am"...

CHAPTER 18

We come as little Children.

As far back as I can remember, and that goes back clearly to the age of seven, I knew I was different from my friends and piers in the neighborhoods and schools. I've always been attracted to my own sex. Yes, even as a child I knew I would never be able to be like them. As I grew older and the hormones kicked in, I would make the effort to bring myself in line to the teachings of the church, but always with a dismal result, and often with rejection. Yet I knew deep down inside I was a good and decent person. The battle went on and on, by the time I was thirty-five, my mind was like a piece of raw meat, battered and bruise buy all the "do gooder's" that wanted to fix me. There was no healing for me till I was forty-five years old. Then I started reading. First was the Ragamuffin Gospel, by Brennen Manning of New Orleans. It was the first time I heard someone speaking the truth. During the following years I had a paradigme shift in my life, and I read every thing I could on the subject. Through constant probing and research I started to meet people that had experienced the same.. I realize now that we came as little children to be with our God, but people held us back, I'm sure they meant no harm, they did the best with what they had been given. But every action they took made me feel guilty, and unclean, and unworthy to approach the throne of Gods grace. Now as I look and read, I see the wonderful love of the Lord, specially as he gathered the little children. He took each one and blessed them, there was no qualifying criteria to be held and blessed by him. The children just believed in him and wanted to come, for that he picked them up and held them one by one and blessed them. More over when he realized that his disciples were trying to keep them away he became indignant, and said to them "Let the children come to me and do not hinder them. It is just such as these that the kingdom of God belongs. I assure you that whoever does not accept the reign of God like a little child shall not partake in it." Then he embraced them and blessed them, placing his hands on them. When we are seeking God, a spiritual life, and a oneness of spirit with him, we too are the children of God. If you feel God calling to you, do not be afraid to run to him. He will pick you up wipe away your tears, and he will allow you to feel the healing power of his grace. He will anoint you with his own blessing, and he will give you the courage to step out and share the truth to our brothers and sisters.

CHAPTER 19

Walking on the waters of life.

esus walked on the waters, and I have often thought about that, reflecting on, what's in this message that applies to this day and age. The thing that keeps coming to mind is not so much the physical action, but that we are called to walk on the waters of life in a spiritual way. Faith itself is a gift, given to us by the father. The first step out on the water spiritually is to accept this gift, to totally receive it into our very being. So many have been offered this wonderful gift and so few have ever accepted it fully. Some have absorbed it intellectually, but things don't happen until its part of your person hood. It is difficult to explain, because the presence of faith in our live doesn't translate well into language. Its more of a living experience.

When you totally accept faith, you are changed in spiritual energy. For one thing you live each new moment as a new creation, totally wiped clean by Gods grace. In living your life in faith there is no guilt sapping away your spiritual energy. You step forth each moment in the secure unending totally encompassing love of the Creator. As you are living in your gift of faith and grace, you are living in the kingdom of god. A person walking in faith and grace is not waiting for the kingdom to show up. He / she is already experiencing a spiritual life as a citizen in Gods kingdom. Your out look on life becomes a positive one. I cannot, for the life of me figure out why any one would choose to live a life full of pain and anguish, as most of this world does, when such peace and harmony are available to every one and its all free. The only explanation I can come up with, is that most people feel they are not deserving of Gods love, taught buy leaders who have totally bypassed the gift that Jesus gave to us on the cross that day.

The gift of Gods unending grace that makes us pure as snow. The Gift of Gods grace is directly united to the gift of faith. When you come to except one, then you get the other as well. When these are embedded into your being, you then are able to step out on the waters of life as a new creation. People that walk in faith and covered with Gods grace radiate spiritual energy. They see the goodness that is in the world. They do not make Judgments about people, groups, community's, or actions, because they know that there but for the grace of God was I. I am calling the entire church to come into a life of faith and grace. It is time now to put down the rocks, back onto their piles, those of you who like the rest of humanity that have not lived up to the life of Jesus.

CHAPTER 20

To right
the un-right-able wrong.

No it is NOT Don Keote' the Man of La'Mancha, Just Ken once more, with more spiritual truth. I've been thinking about those who have been in pursuit of persecuting our community. Those that cant quite seem to focus on reflecting inwardly the clear instructions of Matthew7:1-5. This passage titled Avoiding Judgment says "If you want to avoid judgment, stop passing judgment. Your verdict on others will be the verdict passed on to you. The measure with which you measure, will be used to measure you. Why look at the speck in your brothers eye, when you miss the plank in your own? How can you say to your brother. "let me take the speck out of your eye," while all the time the plank remains in your own? You Hypocrite!! Remove first the plank from your own eye; then you will clearly see to take the speck from your brothers eye. The response is <u>Forgiveness</u>. We are not to let the sun go down on any ill feeling towards any of them. They will heap enough coal on there own shoulders, and have done so already. Which brings me to the saying , (Bear with me now) Be perfect as Christ was perfect. (Now I hear laughter out there), OK. Here is how that is done. We can only be perfect as Christ was perfect, in his unrelenting mercy. This truly is an attainable way of life. Think about it. And this is the way we should and will pull the community up out of the pathetic pit that Society, Family, and Church has tried to bury us in. However, we can pray for their recovery through the restoring of the Gospel of Grace. We as the church can lead Nations back to the true meaning of the Gospel of Grace. The Beatitudes. How blest are the poor in spirit: the reign of God is theirs. Blest to are the sorrowing they shall be consoled. Blest are the lowly; they shall inherit the land. Blest are they who hunger and thirst for Holiness; they shall have there fill. Blest are they who show mercy; mercy shall be theirs. Blest are the single- hearted for they shall see God. Blest too are the peacemakers; they shall be called sons of God. Blest too are those persecuted for holiness' sake; the reign of God is theirs. Blest are you when they insult you and persecute you and utter every kind of slander against you because of me. Be glad and rejoice, for your reward is great in heaven; they persecuted the prophets before you in the very same way..

CHAPTER 21

Strangers in a foreign land.

ave you ever considered how St. Paul must have felt. Lets just think about it for a moment. Paul a Roman military man in direct opposition to the Christian movement, suddenly was converted to a Christian way of life. He saw things quite differently than even some of the Christian leaders of the day, since they wanted the conversion of the Jews the chosen people, even going to the extremes of asking their Christian followers to be circumcised as was the Jewish tradition. Paul felt that Christianity should be shared with the Gentiles as well as the Jews, and there was a great discussion at Antioch. The end result was the conversion of millions of Gentile people to Christianity. The main line Christians did not want the good news shared with the Gentiles. They wanted an exclusive in this spirituality, but because of the courage of St. Paul we Gentiles that profess that we believe in Jesus as our Lord and Savior, have the hope of living as God's people and, enter the kingdom solely in faith. The Church doesn't seem to have changed much from what I can see today, when you consider the plight of the gay community today, millions of people, good loving sensitive gifted spiritual folk who wish to live there lives with god, are made outcasts, closed from the churches simply because they are different in their sexuality. They are gay. Most have tried to come into living their spiritual life, but because most of Christendom wants all to follow age old doctrines and exclusion policies, many gays have given up in despair of trying to follow a conventional Christian life. This book is dedicated to tell the gay community, that as the gentiles were rejected, and that rejection was overcome by St. Paul's steadfast spiritual beliefs and teachings, so to will the gay community be accepted into the Christian realm. We need to believe that

as the Gentiles believed in the resurrection
of Jesus, and their faith in proclaiming Jesus
as their God and savior, brought them into
normalized Christian fellowship, so to will
the gay community of spiritual believers come
into fellowship with the Christian church.
Now there are many gays, that don't want to
put forth a new effort to live a spiritual life
in Jesus. After constant rejection they have
accepted the belief that they do not belong.
They feel like strangers in a foreign land.   It
is time now to follow the decisions at Antioch.
What is good for the Gentiles, is good for not
only gays of faith, but all people of faith. Lets
face it, the Gentiles were a people who had to
walk as strangers in a foreign land, some have
now reached the pinnacle of church leadership,
but they must remember there roots. You were
as rejected as the gay community is today!
You were an alien in the kingdom. So why do
you persecute the gay church?   Gay people of
faith, you must restore your courage, you must
restore your faith , and you must be honest and
acknowledge who you are. Accept this, move
on in life and fearlessly profess your faith, that

all who believe in Jesus are sons and daughters of God, and will have eternal life. Consider this, Jesus didn't say Gentiles can't come into the Kingdom, neither did Jesus say that gays cant come into the kingdom. The only ones that are proclaiming this are, gentiles that have forgotten there roots, forgotten that they are not supposed to judge, forgotten Jesus's Commandment that they are to love others as he loved us. God loves you just the way you are. He loved the thief that died beside him too. All that was required was that he acknowledges Christ as Lord. Jesus remember me when you come into your kingdom, that was his acknowledgment..

CHAPTER 22

Dear Doubting Thomas:

ou were with us all through the last twenty-two messages, and you were wittiness to the word, as it came, all of it directly from scripture. Still, you are hanging on to the security blanket of guilt. If it is because you were brought up to feel guilty, I can understand that. But God wants singers to sing, dancers to dance, teachers to teach, artist's to paint, prophets to prophesy, and God wants lovers to love one another. He wants all his people complete. It is not in Gods plan, that you are not supposed to be you. God does not want you to be held prisoner in a jail that you do not deserve to be in. Now, Tom I want to clear this up once and for all, You can prove it all buy yourself. Please go to your bible and turn to Mark Three. Have you found it yet Tom? Mark comes after Matthew. Have you found it? Mark, Good! Tom, you look at Mark3:28-29 in your very own bible. Tell me Tom, What does it say there? Quote it Tom. "I give you my word, every sin will be forgiven Mankind and all the blasphemies men utter. But who ever blasphemes against the holy spirit will never be forgiven. He carries the guilt of his sin without end." Tom, in the sixty-one years I have lived, never once have I ever heard a man blaspheme the Holy Spirit. N. E. V. E. R. The price is unthinkable. Tom, if you are a believer in Jesus, and he lived a perfect life, do you think that he would lie to you whom he loves. "All sin will be forgiven Mankind". Everything Tom is locked in sin, according to the law. That's why we who believe in Jesus, have to live in faith, not the law. Because it is only through faith that men are justified. The law will not get you into heaven Tom. But faith in Jesus will.

CHAPTER 23

God doesn't make junk.

reat news for the gays that don't think they deserve a spirit filled life.

Please take the time to absorb what you are about to see and experience one line at a time.

The spirit of the Lord is upon me,
because the Lord has anointed me.
He has sent me to bring glad tidings to the lowly,
to heal the broken hearted,
to proclaim liberty to the captives and, to release the prisoners.
To announce a year of favor from the Lord and, a day of

vindication by our God, to comfort all who mourn.

You are a unique one of a kind special precious child of God and there is no one else that carries the spiritual gifts that you do. Today you have been called to reach out across the gay community, and let them know they too have a spiritual life, and are called to use their unique spiritual gifts. Who else will tell them? Who will heal their spiritual wounds? Who will reach out to their gay brothers and sisters?

God doesn't make junk .

Before I formed you in the womb, I knew you, before you were born, I dedicated you, a prophet to the nations, I appointed you.

CHAPTER 24

I'm beginning to see what's hurting the church

It's the way we treat one another,
it's time we all put our judgments
aside, and begin to hug one another
and, spiritual healing will rise like the tide.

A bible verse thrown as a missile I've found,
can pierce the heart through and through,
when we should be directing it inward you see,
that would make God's message ring true.

CHAPTER 25

How blessed we are.

I stop and think, just how blessed we are. The road that most of us have had to travel, the encounters that we've had in an effort to find a true spiritual connection with God. How many times we have searched, and how many times we were not allowed to go in. The big and beautiful churches would not recognize us, and yet there was the longing to come home to our father's house. If it were not set by God in our minds, and in our hearts, and constantly encouraged by the Holy Spirit, we would have been discouraged and given up hope. But God has blessed us, in a very special way. We didn't have church leaders to shine the light on the path. We had to grope our way through the darkness. We had to feel, and experience a lot of the pain that Jesus came to free us from. We saw our friends being rejected also, and with nothing to grasp on to, as they fell deeply into the abyss of spiritual starvation. No light to shine on them to show them, that God loves them. But we have a wonderful God, and he is showing a brilliant light, and that light is shinning down on the Gay community. There is a mighty wind blowing, the rush of the Holy Spirit. It's blowing on us all. No more will there be gatekeepers to select who can receive the Holy Spirit, or who can come into the presents of God. When we hear him call, we can come, we can return to the comfort of our father's endless love. Yes, we have not been invited by an earthly gatekeeper, we have been invited by the Master himself. Because we kept searching, we have been invited into the sanctuary of the Holy Spirit buy Jesus..

CHAPTER 26

Morning meditation

Thanks Lord for giving me another day.

Thanks for my healthy body that I can enjoy life.

Thanks for my wonderful lover and, the care he shows for me.

Thanks for the gift of faith that allows me to walk with you each day.

Thanks for the gift of grace that heals my spirit each moment.

Thanks for the Church family you have blessed me with.

Thank you Lord for my gay personhood, that gives me simpatico with other's.

In Memoriam

Rex says good bye to his beloved community and friends

When I have come to the end of the road, and the sun has set for me, I want no rites in a gloom-filled room; why cry for a soul set free? Miss me a little, but not too long, and not with your head bowed low. Remember the love that we once shared, and miss me, but let me go. For this journey we all must take and each must go it alone. It's all a step in the Master's plan, a step on the road to home. When you are lonely and sick at heart, go to the friends we know. Bury your sorrows in doing good deeds. Miss me, but let me go.

Conclusion

*I*f you have internalized, and absorbed the message in this book, if you are living in the gospel of grace, if you are sharing with others this message, then you are a living Apostle of Jesus serving in the modern day church.

Your testimony on how this book has touched your life, would be greatly appreciated. Please feel free to email me.

I leave you in peace, love, and joy in the Lord.

e-mail   LaFleur2009@aol.com

This book is the perfect gift for the Gay Spiritual Lives, of your Partner, Friends, or their Friends and Families.

www.ingramcontent.com/pod-product-compliance
Lightning Source LLC
Chambersburg PA
CBHW020436290526
45785CB00002B/869